MASSIMO WOLKE
FARTING HORSES
COLORING BOOK

MASSIMO WOLKE
FARTING HORSES
COLORING BOOK

Bibliografische Information der Deutschen Nationalbibliothek:
Die Deutsche Nationalbibliothek verzeichnet diese Publikation in
der Deutschen Nationalbibliografie; detaillierte bibliografische
Daten sind im Internet über http://dnb.dnb.de abrufbar.

© 2018 Massimo Wolke
Herstellung und Verlag:
BoD – Books on Demand, Norderstedt

ISBN: 978-3-7528-3539-7

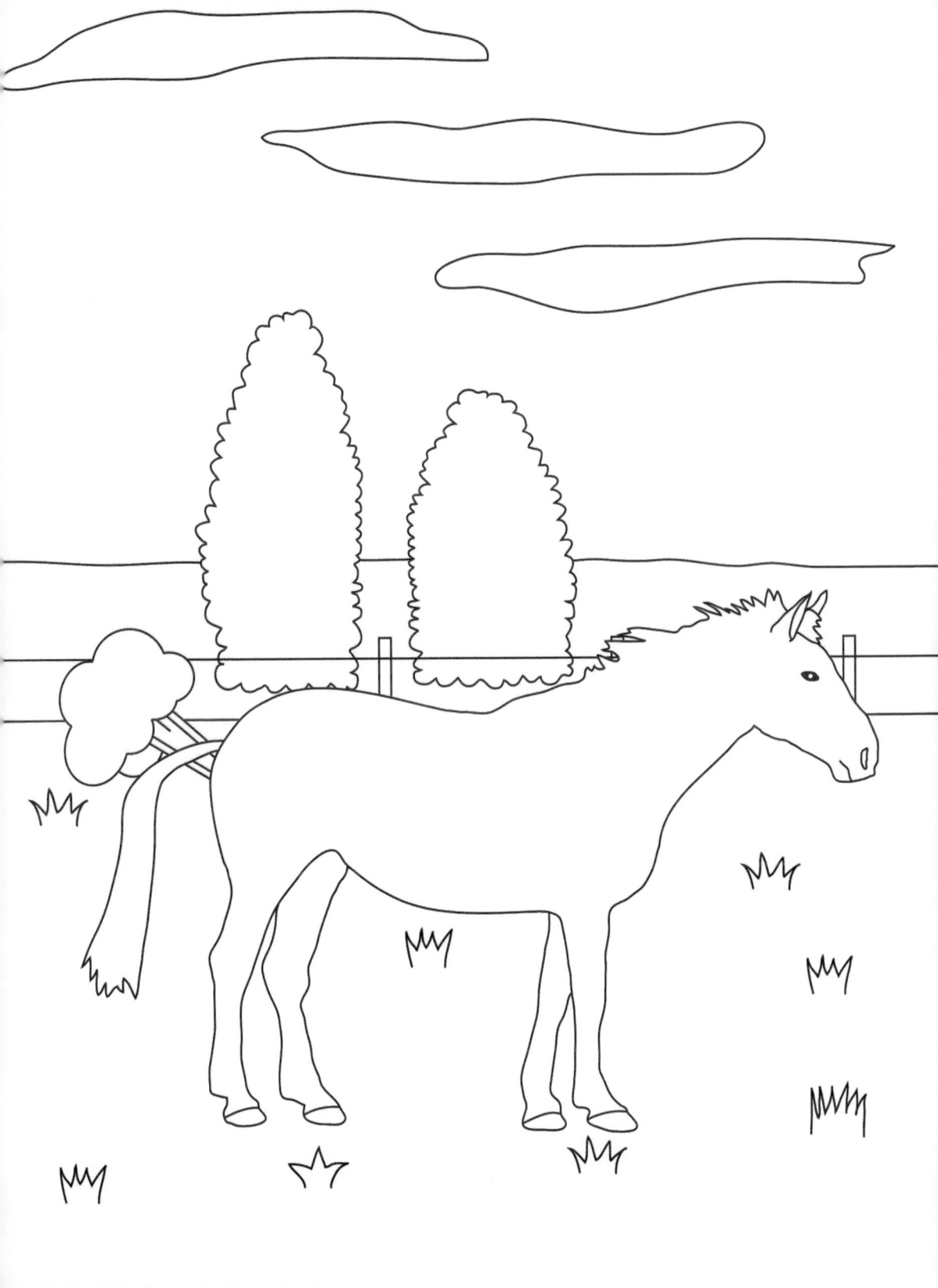